This 'n That

Poetry

Shirley Radcliff Bruton
Debra Davis Hinkle

DacSaysPublishing | San Luis Obispo

Debra Davis Hinkle and Shirley Radcliff Bruton
DacSaysPublishing
San Luis Obispo, CA/93401
dacsayspublishing@pacbell.net

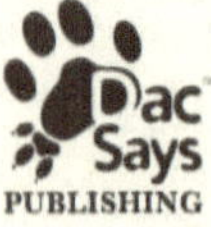

Special discounts are available on bulk purchases, sales promotions, fund-raising, and educational needs. For details, contact the publisher at the email address above.

Publisher's Note: Some of the poetry is memoir in nature. In the poetry we have tried to recreate events, locales, and conversations from our memories of them.

More artistic license is generally accepted in poetry, so each poet is the final editor of her work.

Book Layout by Debra Davis Hinkle 2020
All photos in the paperback are in black & white; they are in color in the eBook.

Editor: Dick Bruton

Cover design by Donna Murphy

This 'n That Poetry/ Debra Davis Hinkle and Shirley Radcliff Bruton. -- 1st ed.
Published in the United States of America.

ISBN-13: 978-0-9884076-7-1 Paperback
ISBN-13: 978-0-9996611-3-0 eBook

*"Dedicated to
the poetic soul
in everyone."*

~ DEBRA DAVIS HINKLE

"Strength lies in differences, not in similarities..."

~ STEPHEN COVEY

Contents

Shirley Radcliff Bruton

She Walked into The Room

Dedicated to Tristan Bruton
Born 2013

She walked into the dimly light room
saltine crackers covered the floor

Fire shot out from the side walls
darting in and out
like a lizard's tongue
hot time tonight

Without hesitation
she stepped on the crackers
crossing over to the other side
monkeys danced on the table tops
giraffes and elephants talked at the bar
bunnies scurried about on the floor

She felt oddly out of sorts,
and wondered who recommended
this place to her and why
she was overdressed

With all eyes on her,
she decided to visit the ladies' room
things quieted down
to a dull whisper

Inside, perched upon a big fluffy pillow
a leopard greeted her
recumbent, submissive, alluring
tilting its head slightly to the left,
and lifting its chin,
as though wanting a scratch,
or a rub; she decided to leave

Gliding, once again,
over the crushed crackers
she danced a soft shoe
to the front door

A gentle turn and she faced the party
blew everyone a kiss,
bowed, and left

Remembering Firenze

Dedicated to Firenze Crawford

Teacher - Mentor - Friend

At first
you loved me
more than I loved myself

You helped me find
the rhythm of my heart
and I journeyed within

I saw leaves dancing in the wind
descend and meld into the earth
only to return again transformed

I saw an ocean's wave
existing but for a moment
and without so much as a glance
life celebrated its beauty and depth

My dear Firenze
I rest in the fullness
of your memory

Mona

Dedicated to the memory
of Mona Schreder

She's gone
it seems too early
but she's gone

The endless struggle to stay connected
like a strand unraveling from a sweater,
you try to catch it in time, to mend the gap,
but the pull is too strong
the edges continue to open wider and wider

We asked ourselves
Was there something more
we could have done to stop the
unraveling,
something that was overlooked?
But she slipped away, from us, from herself and
we had to accept what was/is

When the separation became permanent,
in the stillness of her absence,
the mending shifted from her to us
we opened our hearts to the loss and pain

As our family continues to grow, we slowly
begin to wrap ourselves in new colors,
new designs, new threads

But the older garment
will always be a favorite
its softness feels good against the skin
like a caress of warm memories

Late Afternoon Drive

Rose colors seep in
through my car windows

I'm ensnared by the setting sun
temporarily stained

It spreads slowly across treetops
mingles with greens and browns
changing hues about the landscape

Until the long shadows of dusk move in
and swallows it all up

Understanding Love

Dedicated to 8-year-old Alexi Bruton

I wonder if somehow
we aren't all in love with life
a little more through Alexi
who says, I'm too happy
as he celebrates his dad and *Baby's* wedding

His course of action is different than ours
it's a heightened reality of determination
as he engages his feet, legs and limbs
before he begins to move his walker
down the grassy knoll to the canopy
where he is needed as a groomsman

His generous smile reaches out to us all
touched and elevated by his presence
we witness his grace, gentleness and joy
encourage him and ourselves with lightness of
spirit

He lifts us out of our own boundaries
and shows us there are other ways
to navigate life

We become the flowers
and he the butterfly, fluttering about
accessing flight through his senses

You brought a deeper understanding
of love, my dear Alexi
to this ceremony, to this union
of husband, wife and child

For George

Dedicated to George Arthur Watts
1928-2018
Senior Design Specialist
with a long history in aeronautics
including NASA, Lockheed, and finally as a consultant

I think of outer space as a true continuum
silent
peaceful

A sense of self emerges
empty
full
unknown

Stretching out forever with ease
breathless
fearless
self-reflective
in awe

Thanks for your endeavors
your insights, your kindness
and your time with us

Driving to Santa Barbara

For Cindy

Car lights guide me
through the early morning darkness
and dense fog of canyons and grades

The day takes its time to wake up
the snail's pace is tedious
and tiresome, but finally
it's the sun's turn at the landscape
and everything begins to change

Colors splinter across the cloudy sky
as though an artist dipped her fingers
into jars of paint, and then stroked
the first light of day
her abandon is our pleasure

The extenuation of hues
lie next to each other like lovers
mingle and merge in intense vividness
then separate and disperse

To my right the steaming mist of dawn
coats the fine feathers of sea gulls
(the Zen masters of the beach)
who simply wait and watch
as the salty water licks the shoreline

Santa Barbara is just ahead
and with it a chance to hang with Cindy
sweet

From the Car Window

Up close
a kaleidoscope of colors
whizz by the car windows

Farther out, the stillness
of the hills and the distant trees
offer dark shadows to the landscape

And, higher up
magical, magical clouds
how do you do it
moving into darkness
with so little time left
smearing your hues and shapes
against the evening sky
a brief stain into the wonder of it all

I Miss You Netty

I still see you
dashing down the driveway
belly swishing
stopping to scratch
on your favorite fallen branch

Or, walking through the house
with purpose and determination
hissing
at our boy cats along the way
you preferred the company of dogs

Losing myself to your feline sensuality
petting your fine, silky hairs
purring
you clawed at my cloths
lost in the depths of pleasure

My husband adored you too
understanding
appreciating one another
so sweet, and now so sad

You would follow him into the bathroom
hoping to find him sitting
on the toilet with his pants draped
around his ankles,
a favorite place to nestle

Many years later,
you aged beyond repair,
and the three of us had to say
goodbye
you drifted into euthanasia
we stayed behind in sorrow and loss

I return to your spot on the sofa,
and drink from the remembrances
my throat constricts
my eyes burn
I miss you Netty

Rot

She rots
along the back hillside
bloated, stiff
reeking

With a slow gait
head hanging low
ears flattened
she lay down in a patch of tall oats,
and never rose again
her fawn stayed awhile, then left

Let nature take its course, they said
so, she was left for the buzzards
one came, then two, then more
parked on branches and waited
making sure their meal was ready for them

Dropping down
with large heavy wings
they poked and pulled
became territorial and left unfulfilled
she was too toxic for them
poisoned perhaps

Weeks passed
the stench grew stronger
until it lessened and we could open
windows and the side door again

She's still up there
I look in her direction
staring at her quiet, lifeless body,
and identify in some sad
lonely place I harbor

Perhaps after the winter rains
she'll melt into the earth,
and I'll get the courage to go
and look closely at the details
of her remains, of what's left

My Toe

It wraps around my little toe
like a finely woven scarf
of black with blue streaks

In one quick movement
I grabbed for my foot
crying out, doubled over
How could a wrenched toe hurt so much?

Now I'm forced to be still
rest, move slowly
ice and rest again

I'm shown
my inflated ego
driven by so much to do
with so little time

The Young Buck

In the heat of an August afternoon
he enters
the shade
beneath the bridge of our house

He takes the seclusion he needs
elegant
cautious
the cool earth is inviting

Like a pond reflecting its surroundings
in silence
he settles down
I walk softly above him

What good fortune
in the quiet
of the afternoon
my time with him

Birds, Fish and a Cat

Busy day
late afternoon
exhausted

Shapes drift across my comforter
in wide rows of black and white
against red

Are they abstract images
of birds
or fish?

If they're birds
they could be dead
floating down a river like fish

Hmm ...
slipping
into a catnap

Anger

We're justified, uncompromising,
stubborn. The unfairness, the
insensitive response, the hurt
pulls at us. We speak with the
tongues and breath of dragons.
Our flames burn.

Anchored in anger, we pay
the dues. The loss of a good
friend? — perhaps,
but even that
is in question.

With time, the
temperament
and fervor
lessens.

Can we ever get back to where we were?
Doubtful. But like the shedding of skin, the dust of who we were in anger lies about on the surface of things, a reminder of the cause and effect of our actions.

Darkness

The full-bellied cloud descends
shrouding me
in its dark heavy dampness

Savoring the demise
I carry its sad message of uncertainty,
and fear, like sacred objects,
into the recesses of my soul

The patterns of deception
weave a vibrant tapestry
I wrap myself up in its illusion

Like grains of sand
slipping through my fingers
I disappear quickly
only fragments of who I was
linger behind

How can another know me
when I'm so well hidden
melt down, melt down
the monster is here...

I need someone who's fearless
someone who can sing the demons away
Is it too much to ask?
Is anyone that strong?
Am I?

The Wild Things Are Missing

Wildflowers with their vivid colors
spread out across the hillsides like skirts,
pressing their beauty into the hips
and valleys
sensual, seductive, delightful,
are now missing.

Our creek bed, once full of dandelions,
weeds, native grasses, and wild oats,
rests in a thirsty slumber.

Four years of drought, and the city's lake
is rutted with mounds of dried up
mud, and dead fish.

Ducks and geese and migratory birds pass
overhead, looking for the reflective waters
they once knew.

Searching the arid landscape
for the wild things,
the sun rises and sets, offering an illusion
of dampness within its shadows.

Fine dust clings to my shoes,
as though begging for a handout.

The Mist is Touching Everything

You almost don't see it
then you're so happy you do
the mist is touching everything

In the rich blue light
of early evening
spider webs glisten with moisture

I lift my face to the soft wet haze
my eyes close

I'm sure it must be gathering
on the petals of flowers
slowly rolling off leaves
sliding down branches and tree trunks

Its fullness turns into a steady caprice
seeping deeper and deeper into the ground
Is it caressing earthworms yet?

Waiting for Abundance

yielding their strength
to the heat of the day
low-lying lavender
rests on the ground

parched roots reach out
like arms and legs
crawling in the desert
seeking an oasis

flowers shrivel, brown and dry
they're no longer able to provide
food for the bees
local honey is in short supply

surrendering to the dictates
of the drought,
we wait year after year
accepting, tolerating, modifying
paradigms shift
into a new perception of abundance

He Likes the Pantry Best

Last night, it was the purest,
sweetest sound.
Softly the sax resonated in the distance.

He likes the pantry best.
Jars of dry goods surround him.
Sweets, and nuts tempt him.
"The vibration is best here," he claims.

Coming into the bedroom
with supple, velvety steps,
he saw that I was still up reading.
"Did you catch any of that?" he asked.
I smiled, and said, "It must be the pork pie hat you're
wearing, inspiring and placing you with your muse."
He smiled back,
lifting his hat and tilting his head.

A Simple Misunderstanding

A simple misunderstanding
expands into a heart-wrenching
soul demoralizing growth.

I look out at my garden,
it feels cold, abandoned.
Sunlight streaks randomly
across the frigid morning.

Then you wash the window
to my room. The bugs, dust and
unknown smudges are wiped away.

I feel ready to start anew.
What just happened?
An observation,
a reflection,
on us, or life?
Am I able to separate the two?

Quietly, Carefully

Quietly, carefully he steps
foraging *boletus*
feeding the wild turkeys and birds
providing the deer with a salt lick
encouraging life

Except for the monocots, thistles
and burclover; he tracks them down
relentlessly, extracting them without
disturbing the surrounding grasses

Bent over, distracted by his quest,
his mission knows no boundaries
wandering into other yards
helping out our neighbors
who could care less

He always pauses to look skyward
at the sound of birds or planes
acknowledging their uniqueness

A Gift

Is there a breath left in you
lying there so limp

The tip of my little finger
strokes your soft speckled belly
and your snowy white-tipped tail feathers
gently tracing the iridescent greens, blues
and reds
that once wedded the afternoon sunlight

Did one of our felines
again take her nature to heart
bringing us a special gift

I wish I could re-gift this one
back into the day

Displayed and read at
"Animal Friends in Art and Poetry" exhibit
Atascadero Library
San Luis Obispo County
Spring 2019

Silence

Ah, the pool of silence
washes over me

Droplets of peace gather in my heart
and pulse down my veins

Its moisture reaches my feet
releasing wet footprints
as I walk

You Know

Part of a conversation I overheard on my morning walk as I passed in front of a porch. It was between a mother and her daughter, but I only heard the daughter's voice. It was strong and pleading. The mother's too soft to hear. There was a baby crying, in an undemanding way, almost cooing.

You know
it's like I do the best I can

I don't know
my schedule is so full

I mean
I guess I could make more time

But then
you know

It's like
I rarely have time
to do the things I have to do
every day is so full

You know

    I mean

        I don't know

            It's like

I do the best I can

Canopy of Blossoms

A canopy of blossoms
sweep up into each other's arms
tickling, supporting, embracing
one another in the abundance
of Spring

We step beneath the ephemeral intimacy
our feet glide light and easy
on the weightless fallen petals that rocked back
and forth on their descent
to more earthly gains

Inhaling radiating sweetness,
we become part of the exhibition
a site-specific installation,
ever changing,
artist unknown, and yet known to all

Night Sky

Inside my private darkness
I open the front door
and step out into the breath of night

Glancing up at the sky
I toss myself out into the universe
like the stars

No longer limited
by time
or circumstance

The night sky
offers a brief reprieve
from my finite mind

Egret

You fly in from afar
strong, broad-breasted
propelling your wings forward
as though swimming
through the air that surrounds you
long legs trail behind your coveted feathers

Sweeping down into familiar territory
you enter the low-lying wetlands
of your Arcadian heritage

Plopping and squishing in the mud
you carefully wade and probe,
with the patience of your lineage

A quick — rapid — thrust,
and a catch is made
pierced by your beak
held tightly

Satisfied, you spread your massive wings
like a ballet dancer, and rise
with water dripping from your feet
becoming a sliver in the
afternoon twilight

Gazing into the placid, reflective
waters of the marsh, I wonder
Who is the observer, and who is the observed?

So Quiet

A hush surrounds the old oak trees
green leaves darken
into an outline
of their former selves

In the blue evening light
a bird
quickly pushes
through the air currents
to get back home

In the darkness of the night
I hear the sound of my breath
the pulsing of my heart
so sweet, so quiet

Rocks

Rocks full of color
rest beneath the water's cool surface

Frogs jump their plumpness
from rounded edge to rounded edge

Sleek, angular dragonflies
maneuver the air
like puppets on a string

Look under the rocks, she advised
and I did

Found any gold yet? he joked
and I did

To dream the day away
at the shore's edge
is a desire highly sought after

To discover yourself amongst rocks
is the dream come true

It's Going to Rain

The sun claims the afternoon
for as long as it can
but ever thickening clouds
cover the sun with a dark grey mass

For a brief moment
the sun is allowed back in
slanting rays take center stage
birds welcome the drama in song

But the eclipsing darkness
upstages it once more,
and everything is quiet again

Now, it's going to rain

Fog

Fog pulls its silence
from the sea

Singular and vast
a thick wetness drifts onshore

The pier stretches out
to greet it

Creating a new expression
of what was, and still is

Pine Trees

Up high, in the Mother Lode,
where veins of gold
drew so many, rest quaint homes,
attracting tourists seeking a respite from
the city's
clamoring demands.

Just before dawn, and
during the earliest hours of the morning,
we hear the birds sing.
Then the distant chorus of chain saws
arrive.

I see through our kitchen window, felled
pine trees stretching
silently over the ground, marooned,
docked, locked into place.
Their round expressionless faces stare
back at me.

Side by side they rest, as though
sunning at the beach,
like lovers, one on top of the other,
or strewn about, like pickup sticks.

The pine's pitch flows no more.
Inner rings of stillness bake in the
noonday,
offering what is left of a drying scent.
The aroma is oddly uplifting and
refreshing.

The winter's cold wet snow passed by
year after year.
Like a train unwilling to stop, or having
stopped,
was a hesitation at best.

Their thirst grew and they became
stressed, alienated,
and diseased.

With its blue stain fungus, the Mountain
Pine Beetle
found the perfect home. Excelling in its
proficient attack
on old and weakened trees. It no longer
was able
to be an eco-friendly neighbor.

Red needles alerted them to a job well
done
and they moved on and on and on
decimating acres.

Huge logging trucks carry the trees, now
just wood,
laboriously up and down the state
highways, spewing fumes,
grinding gears, slowing down traffic.

First to the mills,
then into their final alteration
as chairs, paneling, support beams,
and chipped particle boards.

Out of the forest, and
into the city they go.

Through the Greenhouse Window

In the fall
we drape an old-white-tattered cloth
over the greenhouse
for warmth

Stepping inside, I notice
a small window is barely propped open
I reach up to close it and decide instead
to lift it higher, the morning's
cool damp air greets me

I see a raven's
black silk wings
spread out in flight
she scans the ground below
tilting her massive body
ever so slightly

We soar together
high above the treetops
she searches
I imagine

Debra Davis Hinkle

Nocturnal Guardian

Sunlight shows his
magnificent height and breadth.
His limbs coated with
intensely dark green-black thick fur
and wind-strewn brown decay.

His true nature and purpose
is not perceptible
or even plausible
during the light of day.

Every night he's standing sentry
in the shadows,
near but not reachable.
Each time I see him
from my hot tub,
I'm both thrilled and amazed.

Over time, I become
keen to know him
and deeply comforted by
his presence, his grandeur
and his silent show of strength.

His eyes are lighter
than his fur.
His shaggy mane is
tremendous
in depth and width.

He's a little scruffy around his head
from battles lost and won.
Only a fool
would challenge him now.

When I squint my eyes, I sometimes
think he resembles an enormous tree,
and then he growls or purrs
and all mystification is lost.

Waiting

Waited 900 days,
less than patiently.

Lifetime feral—
you choose to
be with me.

One evening—
came inside,
jumped on my bed,
walked around.
Even marched and
lay down
momentarily.

Jumped down—
I felt like crying,
patted bed,
jumped back up.

Accepted love,
crawled on me,
purred.
Fell asleep—
trust.

Never betray—
time will build
more.

Patience,
hopefully not another 900 days

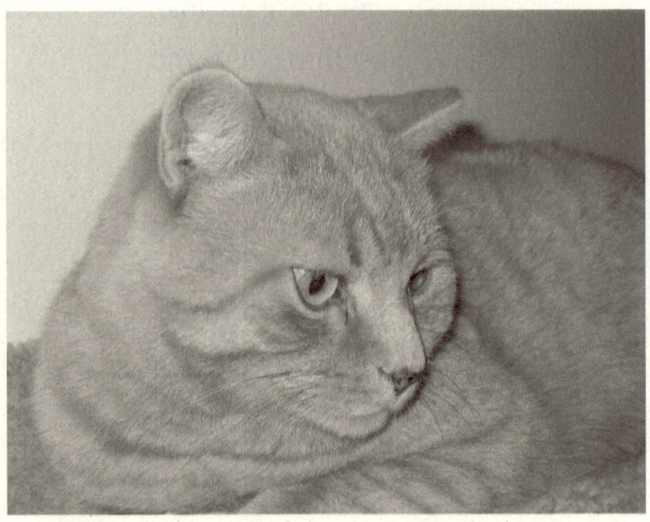

BigBoy on the top of the cat tree in the house.
©Neonesque Artwork by Debra, the cat lady.

Monastic Lizard

Met a little lizard today
in the backyard of
Monastery of the Risen Christ.

Crawled up a bench,
greeted me without fear.

Put out my finger for him to smell.
Asked him if it was okay to touch him,
I stroked his back.

Asked him if he was thirsty,
poured him some punch—
he tasted it only once.

We continued together—
he running and me walking,
he listening and me talking.

Sadly, I had to depart—
me walking, and
he waiting
for the next visitor.

HELMET HAIR

If you skate,
bike, your horse,
ride, *have helmet hair.*
you skateboard,
If you dive.
sky
ride a scooter, you,
too, *helmet hair.*
have
sometimes,
without the fun
or the sweat
from exertion,
you still wake up with
helmet hair.
Damn those
NIGHTMARES.

Some of Life's Struggles

It's a battle—
not just right now,
not even tomorrow
or next year.
A lifetime.

For me
it's a learning disability
or two
or three.
For you
it's...

Anger or acceptance
depending on the day
or whatever.
It's your choice.

Work like hell.
Grow and learn.
If not,
what then?

Invisible

My sister said,
"The camera was so bad,
I didn't even know
you were in the picture."

Just like when
I was a child.
There, but
not there.
Invisible, still.

I'm not invisible and
neither are you.

Always remember,
invisibility
is in the
mind
or
eyes
of another.

His Hands. No, My Hands

Looking down at my hands,
what do I see?
His hands—
large, powerful and mean.

Why do I see his hands,
and not mine?
Is he in my hands,
or
still in my head?

His hands I see,
when I should see mine.
Thank God,
I no longer feel his hands.
I feel my hands, now.
When will I see my hands?
When I no longer remember the pain?

Looking down at my hands
finally, I see
my hands by determination
and time—
wrinkled, strong, powerful,
but kind.

Updated from poem published in
Women's Press, July & August 2009

My Mother

"Be patient toward all that is unsolved in your heart..."

Why did she die at seventy-five?
How old will I be when I die?
Will I see her again?
        God, I hope so.
Does she know how much I loved her?
        I hope so.
Does she know how much I miss her?
        I hope not.
Does she miss me?
        I hope not.
Does the bond die when she does?
        I know it doesn't!

"...try to love the questions themselves..."

With thanks to Rainer Maria Rilke
"Letters to a Young Poet"
First and last lines

Suppose and Unfortunately

Suppose I could do it
all over again—
I would,
in a nanosecond.

To meet him,
again—
fall in love.
I'd leave out a few things, though—
stupid arguments,
midnight cookie runs
to name two.
Add a thing or two, I'm sure—
more exercise for one.

Someone I will never be again—
young—
unfortunately.

Heart to Heart

For Roland, always and forever

I hear it
from his deep heart's essence,
sounds so softy told,
to me alone.

Would it not be louder still?
Sounds so softly told
others would behold.

He hears it
from my deep heart's essence,
sounds so softy told,
to him alone.

Would it not be quieter still?
Sounds so softly told
we would not behold
our deep hearts' souls.

Questions and Answers

Have you ever?
Sat at your mother's bedside as she lay
dying?
Fortunately, yes.
Tamed a wild cat?
Scars to prove it.
Taught your niece and nephews how to
give butterfly kisses?
Luckily, yes.
Found yourself rushing through bath time
with your young nephew?
Only once.
Heard applause?
Yes, I finally did.
Gotten the chance to right a wrong?
Fortunately, yes.
Not always, though.

Withheld forgiveness, while waiting for an apology or a repayment?

Yes, for decades.
When forgiveness came,
the realization that it doesn't
matter whether they *are worthy*
of forgiveness or not.

If you don't like the answers, the first time through—change the answers next time.

Betrayal

Betray a child—
physically,
emotionally,
or
sexually—
betray humanity.

Let someone betray
your child—
physically,
emotionally,
or
sexually—
betray your child.

Betray *your* child—
physically,
emotionally,
or
sexually—
betray *your* humanity.

Buttons

The light filters
through the thin lace
and
reflects back
from the layer
of white silk.

The pearl buttons
run down the back
of my dress
ending
at my slim waist.

But I will never
wear this
breathtakingly beautiful dress,
for my fiancé,
lies motionless
at my feet,
cheated of future breaths.

You see,
iridescent rainbow
glass buttons
aren't the same as
pearl buttons.

He was stupid to
think I wouldn't
recognize the tacky button
from my maid's dress,
that he unconsciously ran
through his fingers,
like a worry stone.

I saw my maid,
yesterday, in town
wearing
a blue dress
with those
cheap
glass buttons.

Through the
window in the
store front,
I saw him touch her arm.

She wasn't
even cultured enough
to care that the top
button was missing
or that he belonged to another.

After all,
I'm a lady,
and
a lady
knows quality
when she sees it.

Everything would have been
perfect if he had
just worried
a little
more about
his fiancée,
me.

Socks

My socks begin with
just one stitch cast on
times forty-eight.
Four double needles that seem like eight—
ten fingers that feel like twenty.
Two weeks stretched into six.
Only one pair of socks, not four.

Knit one, purl one for the cuffs.
Knit two, purl two for the legs.
Knit one row, purl one row for the heel flaps.
Knit and knit together to turn the heels.
Watch the instructor do the gusset.
Knit the feet.
Knit and knit together for the toes.
Cast off by grafting.

Then do it all again.
My twenty-four dollar —
pair of socks.

Take the *Gifts* Life Gives

My mother told me,
not too long before she died,
"You're a wonderful woman
because of what you went through."

"I would rather be a fucking bitch,
than have lived through what I did,"
I responded.
How immature I was to think and say that—
young in years and spirituality.

"Mom, if this was a test—
I finally passed—
you were right
I possess the *gifts* of
great empathy and understanding—
earned the hard way—
through child abuse."

"And, I have long since forgiven you
for not stopping the abuse.
This doesn't mean it was okay
to let your husband abuse me.
It means I have forgiven—
not forgotten.
I will always carry the *gifts*
and the *scars*."

"At the time,
I thought you were making
an excuse for your
enabling the situation.
Now I know,
I was still carrying venom—
when you said I was
a wonderful woman,
you meant I was kind,
sensitive, empathic and
so much more—the *gifts*."

"It is a little late,
but thank you
for the compliment"

"And, *I know*!
Just kidding, Mom."

You're a Real Cowgirl Now

Kick horse.
Horse spook.
Butt hit ground.

I hurt.
Chiropractor—
SNAP
CRACK
POP.
Doctor—
poked,
x-ray.
Pharmacist—
fill bottles.

I still hurt.
Physical therapist—
rub
rub
rub some more.

Do I really want to be a cowgirl?

The Lost Soul

Rescued a horned lizard
from the ***jaws and claws***
of a feral cat.
Placed the reptile
on a bed of leaves.

Re-hydrated an earth worm
twisting
in the ***blazing***
summer sun.
Safely buried under soil.

Found a lost soul
searching
surrounded by friends
and light,
went to the source.

Now they are together,
the *rescuer and the soul.*

Fiola

"Want kitten."

"You're a Fiord.
Can't have kitten."

"Want kitten."

"I'll get you a donkey."

"Want kitten."

"Heehaw.
Heehaw."

"Damn that donkey.
Want kitten."

"Heehaw.
Heehaw."

"Hate donkeys.
Want kitten."

"Okay—
two kittens."

"Heehaw", Fiola says.

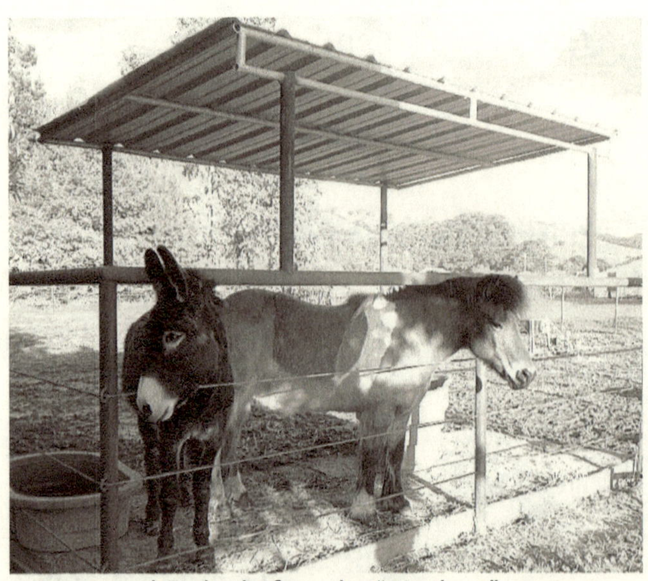

Moca and Fiola, before the "*Heehaw*" moment.

Yet to Come?

She doesn't
want to live
in
the real world.
It's scary
and
painful.

She tries to live
in
the fantasy world
she created.

She's now a
senior citizen
and getting
older, faster.

The first
derivative is
negative
and

the second
derivative is
positive.

Her life is
waning
and she is
sad.
She misses things
that are
lost
or
gone.
She fears the future.

She's dying.

She Misses

His
eyes
that sparkle and dance.

His
squeezes,
hugs and kisses.

His
rough hands
that caress so gently.

Where is her husband?

She feels half-alive.
Without her man,
is she woman?

Time Tells All

Feel the passing of time—
creaks and groans of
muscles and bones
now the reason I moan.

Heavier—
more fat, not muscle,
carried by aging being.

Doctors—
need them:
preventative care,
sick,
and
aging.

She Walked With Me

I had a **tall** *doll*,
almost my size.
When I held her hand
and
swung her arm,
she walked alongside me.

When I needed one,
she became
my friend.

She couldn't take away
my screaming,
from the pain of abuse.
Or even stop the yelling.

But, having a friend,
helped me—
made me feel less alone.

She made me feel loved—,
just a little.

My **tall** *doll*,

Kaye,
that walked the hall
with me.

The Encounter

Long jet-black silky nightgown.
Lace bodice and four spaghetti straps
crossed in the back on bare flesh.

Wine-colored statin sheets,
freshly washed and
turned back in anticipation.

Lightly scented candle
glowing from fluted-champagne crystal,
reflected in the mirror.

She hears the rattle of his keys, finally.
And then his footsteps in the hallway.
He pauses in the doorway to their bedroom.

She jumps on the king size mattress,
promptly sliding across the slippery surface,
down the raised platform bed—
all the way to the floor
on the other side of the bed.
That was not quite what she had planned.
But he was kind enough not to laugh.

Looking back, maybe it wasn't kindness,
something more fundamental.

Hot Tub Afternoon

Hear the rustle of the leaves,
see the movement, too.
Listen to their chatter,
watch the birds soar.
Hear the meows
and see the cats.

See half-moon,
feel the sun's warmth.
See the blue sky,
breathe the clean air.

Airplanes have fluffy
white con trails.
Dispersed in
movement of air,
way above,
based on temperature.

The space station is
brighter than satellites.
Fast moving,
disappears suddenly.

All these things I
see and hear from
my big bathtub
while floating
in my hammock.

When it comes alive
only sight remains.
Hearing gets drowned out
by mechanical noises—
of pump and...

Connection

I wish
I had
children.

Why?
That connection
to my mom,
my sisters
and
to me.

That's what
I want.

It's not *children*
like all *children* would
provide that missing thing.

It's what my mother had.
I want it.
The way I loved
my mom
and
she loved me.

She worked and earned it,
though.

Would I have been able
to do what was necessary
to get what I want now?

It would have been
about the child
or children,
not about me.

Otherwise it's just
a selfish desire.

Letting Go

Sometimes,
letting go
is not only
appropriate
it's the
healthy
thing to do.

One-sided
relationships
are draining
and
ultimately,
they're
not
sustainable.

After
the
confusing
self-doubt
stage,
it's easier
to
move on
without
them.

It does hurt
to lose someone
or
the idea of
losing
the
friendship.

The Train Trip

The train **rocks**, *rolls*,
and *rumbles*.
The familiar **hum**
is soothing.
But, I have never taken
this *exact* trip before.

I have taken this trip
many times
to visit my mother.
We shop and care for
my young nephews.

Many times
I have taken this trip
escorting my nephews
to my home.
Another visit
and more memories.

This trip I have
taken many times.
To care
for my ailing mother.
I am exhausted.

I hoped
never
to take this final trip.
My mother is dead.
I am numb
with grief.

I have taken this trip
to visit my sister,
many times.
I miss my mother less
when I am
with my sister.

I will never
take this trip again.
My nephews
are too old to visit.
My sister is moving
far away.

The train **rocks**, *rolls*,
and *rumbles*.
The familiar movements' **hum**
is soothing.
A new journey unfolds.

Many times
I have taken this trip.
To see my Uncle Bob.
It is always special,
for I am his favorite.

My Uncle Bob
died.
He was all that was left
for me
in Los Angeles.

The train no longer
rocks, *rolls*,
and *rumbles* for me.
There is no
familiar movements' **hum**
for me.
A new journey unfolds
at home,
but not on a train.

Poem first published in Tears to Laughter, Embracing the Future Without Letting Forgetting the Past.
Published by Dac Says Publishing, 2013
Updated for this publication.

Heighten/Overloaded Senses

(Attention Deficit Disorder)

"...riot of **color** and motion..."
Swirl, *blink,* and dance
Random, pattern, chaotic
Little **aura** **migraine** makers
Sense of SIGHT
invaded

Incoming bombs of **racket**
Voices, music, any sound
Harmonic, rhythmic, melodic
Or **not**
Sense of hearing

assaulted

Intense odors
Body, cologne, perfume
Or rotting ***garbage***
Pleasant or nauseating
olfactory senses

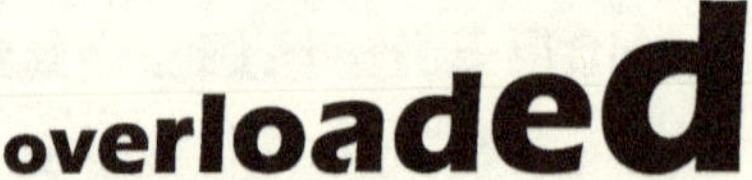

First Line of poem from:
"9 Dragons"
by Michael Connelly

The last two lines were changed after the QR code was made.

About the Authors

Shirley Radcliff Bruton

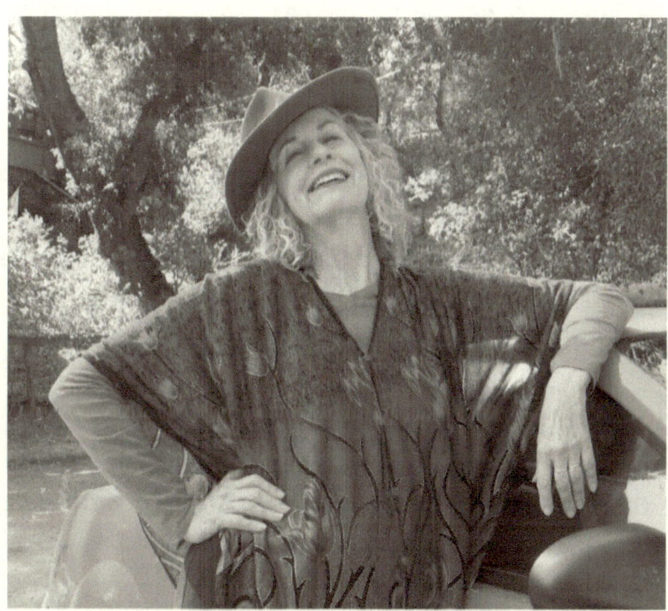

Photo by Marv Lyons

Shirley Radcliff Bruton is a poet, performance artist, and fiction writer.

Her poems about nature are often thought of as noteworthy, the dedications and reflections on people and situations heartfelt, and then there's an occasional flight of fantasy.

As a performance artist, she scripts, stages and directs interdisciplinary artists, along with unskilled performers, to convey her conceptual narratives. Bruton often uses rear projected, magnified photographs, as a backdrop to her performances. They examine things up close, like woven fabric, sections of the human body, insects, moss, etc. When using the subtleties of black and white photography, like shadows (often an image in her poems), they become an entrance into another realm. Shirley has performed both in California and New York City. She is currently working on two short stories and a Chapbook of a performance piece — a work-in-progress.

Shirley Radcliff Bruton lives with her husband Richard (a.k.a. Dick), their cat Muffie, roaming deer, flying, bathing and nesting birds, and other creatures who wander above and below ground. She is a member of the Friday Night Writers' Group — a writing critique group started in 2008.

Finding Shirley:

Facebook: Shirley Radcliff Bruton

Shirley's Amazon Author Page

Shirley's Website
shirleyradcliffbruton.fridaynightwritersgroup.com

Shirley's performances read as poems or prose, both within her notes and spoken scripts. This work is not traditional theatre, but rather random, succinct moments seen as collages within a story. "Shirley Henderson (a.k.a. Radcliff Bruton), poet, philosopher, dancer is equally at home with visuals ..." Diana Zlotnick, *Newsletter on the Arts.*

Debra Davis Hinkle

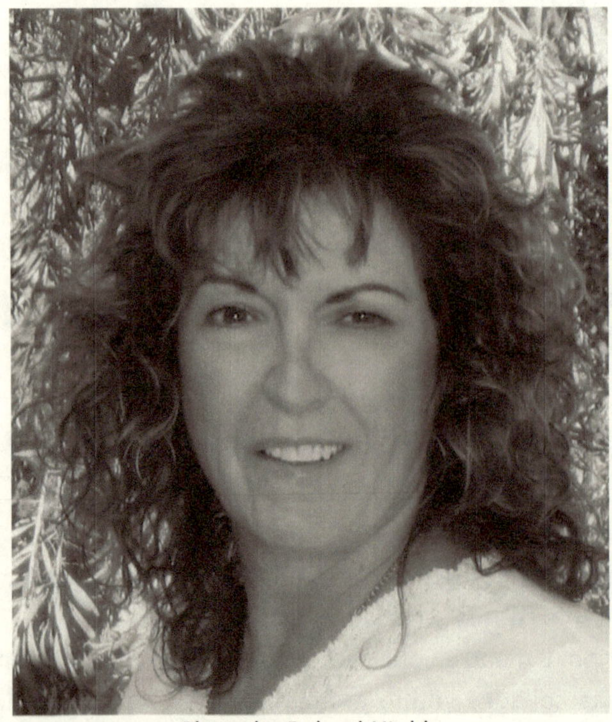

Photo by Roland Hinkle

Poet, author and artist Debra Davis Hinkle grew up in Manhattan Beach, California and currently lives in San Luis Obispo with her husband. She loves animals and has six cats, three are feral, and a dog.

She graduated with a Bachelor of Science from California State University, Long Beach, in Business with emphasis in Information Systems. She has taught computer classes, built websites and was the past Webmaster for SLO NightWriters.

Debra has been writing prose for fifteen years and poetry for twelve. She specializes in creative non-fiction and has numerous awards, including the Lillian Dean First Page Contest several times and The SLO NightWriters Short Story contest.

Her short stories have been published in Tales from the Corner, An Anthology, published by Central Coast Press. Debra's poems have been published in the Tribune and Women's Press.

Debra co-authored a book on bereavement in 2013. She has three books in the works. Her work is available at www.amazon.com.

Debra is a founding member and leader of the Friday Night Writers' Group—a writing critique group started in 2008.

Finding Debra:

Facebook: Debra Davis Hinkle
Goodreads and LinkedIn

Amazon Author Page

Debra's Website
debradavishinkle.fridaynightwritersgroup.com

fridaynightwritersgroup.com

Spokescat

"Hooman, thanks for buying the book; please leave a review."

~Ebony Renfield Hinkle

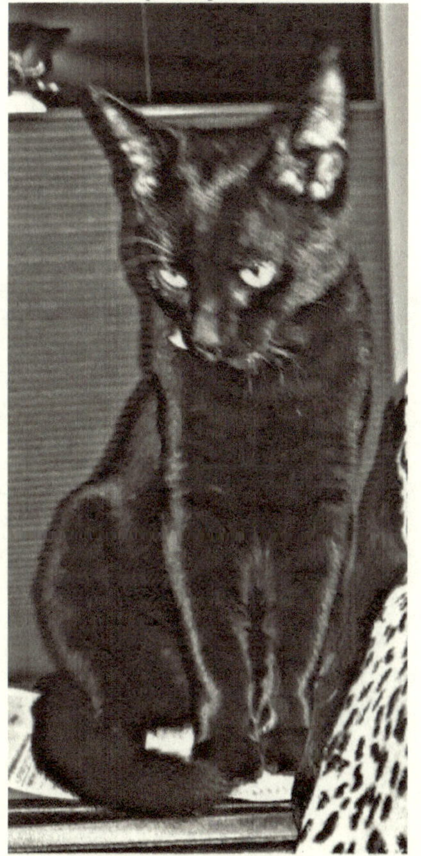

©Neonesque Artwork by Debra, the cat lady.

www.ingramcontent.com/pod-product-compliance
Lightning Source LLC
LaVergne TN
LVHW091009080826
845145LV00003B/1198

* 9 7 8 0 9 8 8 4 0 7 6 7 1 *